The Patchsmith's
SUMMER FUN MUG RUGS

by Amanda Weatherill

SUMMER FUN MUG RUGS
Text and Pattern copyright © 2023 Amanda Weatherill
Paperback Edition Published: April 2023
All rights reserved.
No part of this publication may be reproduced, stored in retrieval system, copied in any form or by any means, electronic, mechanical, photocopying, recording or otherwise transmitted without prior permission in writing from the author.

The designs and projects in this book are copyright but can be made for sale without prior permission from the author, Amanda Weatherill, provided the projects are handmade and credit is given to the author. No mass production allowed.
The information given in this book is presented in good faith. The author has made every effort to ensure that the instructions in this book are accurate. Please study the instructions and diagrams for the pattern you wish to make. However, no warranty is given, nor results guaranteed as responsibility cannot be taken for the choice of fabric, tools, human error or personal skill.

CONTENTS

GENERAL INSTRUCTIONS 1

HINTS AND TIPS 7

MUG RUG PATTERNS

WATERMELON MUG RUG 9

FLOWER GARDEN MUG RUG 13

ICE CREAM SUNDAE MUG RUG..17

TICKER TAPE MUG RUG 21

LIGHTHOUSE MUG RUG 25

BUTTERFLY POCKET MUG RUG..29

TOPIARY TREES MUG RUG 33

LADYBUGS MUG RUG 37

HARBOURSIDE MUG RUG 41

BEACH HUTS MUG RUG 47

ABOUT THE PATCHSMITH 51

General Instructions

Before you start
Read through all instructions for the pattern of your choice before beginning.
Fabric requirements and cutting directions are given at the beginning of each pattern. I give the cutting measurements in the format of "width x height" throughout to help if you wish to fussy cut any pieces.
All seam allowances are ¼" and are included in cutting sizes.
Press seam allowances towards the darker fabric if pressing to one side. Alternatively, you may prefer to press your seams open unless stated otherwise in the pattern.

Using the patterns
Each pattern has been created as a stand-alone unit to allow you to work quickly and easily. The appliqué diagrams are located with the individual patterns and are at the correct size. Some of the appliqué images have been reversed – you should trace them exactly as shown on the appliqué page – they will be the right way round on your finished mug rug.

Fabric Choices
I find choosing fabric takes longer than making the actual mug rug and this is true whether choosing from a designer range or using up scraps left over from a bigger project. The largest piece of fabric you will require for any of the projects in this book is 12" x 8" and that is for the backing - the appliqué detailing uses much smaller pieces. Before you start, make sure any fabric you use is colour-fast (you can test it by soaking a small piece in a bowl of water – the water should remain clear).

If you are new to mug rugs or small quilts then a good way to build up a fabric stash is to use pre-cuts i.e. charm packs and layer cakes. These can be found in most quilting and fabric shops and at craft fayres and exhibition stalls. You will also need a few fat-quarters (quarter of a yard) for background and backing. A good background fabric will have a small print and not be too bold in design or colour.

Do not neglect the back of your mug rug either. This is particularly important if you are creating the mug rug as a gift. Try to choose a backing fabric that will complement the front of the mug rug. Novelty fabrics work well in this respect.

Appliqué

All patterns in this book use the quick and easy fusible method of appliqué. You will need lightweight fusible webbing (i.e. Bondaweb, Vleisofix, Wonderweb or similar). Each pattern includes appliqué instructions but here they are in a little more detail:

1. Trace around the appliqué shapes onto the paper side of the fusible webbing. Fusible webbing has two sides – one smooth (paper side) and one rough (webbing side). Trace the design onto the smooth paper side.
Note: Some of the shapes have been reversed – trace them exactly as shown.

2. Cut out the shapes roughly (do not cut out accurately at this stage). You should leave approximately ¼" free around each shape when cutting out.

3. Follow the manufacturer's instructions to iron the fusible webbing cut outs onto the WRONG side of your chosen fabrics. The rough (webbing) side should be facing the WRONG side of your fabric and you will be ironing the paper side. DO NOT IRON THE WEBBING SIDE – YOU WILL RUIN YOUR IRON.

4. Allow the fabric to cool completely before cutting out the shapes accurately along the traced lines.

5. Peel the paper away from the fusible webbing/fabric.

TIP: *If you have difficulty peeling the paper away from the fabric, scratch the paper gently with a pin until you create a tear in the paper. Slide the pin between the fabric and paper. You should then be able to remove it easily.*

This will leave a layer of glue on the fabric cut outs. Position the fabric cut outs, with the glue side facing down, onto the RIGHT side of the mug rug. Use the appliqué sheet and photo as a guide to their placement and make a note of any pieces which overlap. When happy with the arrangement, fuse the pieces in place according to manufacturer's instructions.

TIP: *Always leave enough room between the appliqué and the edge of the mug rug to allow for binding.*

6. Finally stitch the appliqué shapes securely in place by hand or machine. You can use a running stitch, blanket stitch or any decorative stitch you prefer. It is important to stitch the pieces so that they do not come off when the mug rug is laundered.

Quilting

Mug rugs can be quilted with any thick material you have to hand – it doesn't have to be batting or wadding. You can use old towelling, wool fabric, flannel or interfacing. Whatever you use though should be washable and thick enough to protect the table from hot cups/liquid. I use both natural and synthetic materials ranging in thickness from 2 oz to 4 oz.

When it comes to quilting the finished mug rug, you can make it as simple or as complex as you like, whether by machine or by hand. You can even leave the mug rug un-quilted if you wish.

To prepare your mug rug for quilting, lay the backing material with WRONG side facing up, lay the batting on top and finally lay the mug rug with RIGHT side facing up on top of both. (In effect you have a sandwich of batting between the backing material and the mug rug top.) Baste or pin all three layers together, ensuring that the backing and top remain flat and smooth. Quilt as preferred (hand or machine) and quilt around any appliqué shapes.

Tip: The closer your quilting is to the appliqué shape will determine how 'puffed up' the appliqué is. Try stitching very close (almost touching) and then try ⅛" away on another mug rug and see the difference.

Once all quilting has been completed, trim the backing and batting level with the mug rug top.

Binding Methods

There are many different ways to finish your mug rugs. For all the patterns within this book I have used 1¼" wide cotton strips for binding but you could use bias binding if you prefer. I do not cut my binding on the bias unless I want a particular look i.e. a diagonal stripe. All binding is cut from ordinary quilters' cotton fabric.

You can use any binding method you are familiar with or prefer. There are some excellent tutorials on-line for machine and hand binding. I have given instructions here for simple 'single fold' and mitred binding.

Single Fold Binding

1. Cut four binding strips each measuring 2" longer than the sides of your mug rug i.e. if your mug rug is 6" x 9" cut two 8" and two 11" strips.

2. With RIGHT sides together stitch a binding strip to the top and bottom of your mug rug. Trim excess binding to match width of mug rug. Press the binding away from the mug rug.

3. Repeat with the two remaining binding strips to the sides of the mug rug. Trim excess binding to match length of mug rug. Press the binding away from the mug rug.

4. Fold the binding round to the back of the rug. Turn under ¼" on the outside edge of the binding and slip stitch the binding in place. Be careful not to stitch through to the front of the rug.

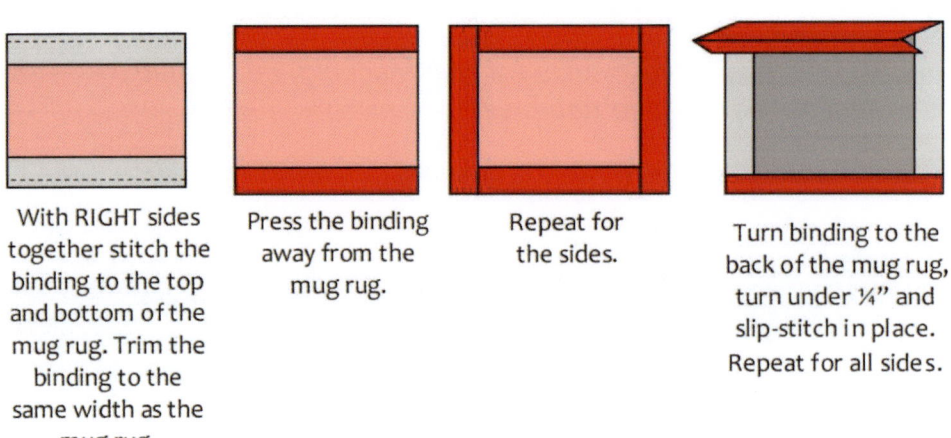

With RIGHT sides together stitch the binding to the top and bottom of the mug rug. Trim the binding to the same width as the mug rug.

Press the binding away from the mug rug.

Repeat for the sides.

Turn binding to the back of the mug rug, turn under ¼" and slip-stitch in place. Repeat for all sides.

Mitred Binding

This method of binding creates a mitred corner finish for your mug rug.
Note: You will need one continuous length of 1¼" wide binding – this can be constructed from strips sewn together. You will find the length of binding required for each pattern in the Fabric Requirements section at the start of the pattern.

1. Fold the short end of your binding strip into a triangle and align to one edge of the mug rug, RIGHT sides together, as shown (this will create a neat start/finish to your binding). Stitch the binding to the side of your mug rug but stop when you are ½" away from the first corner. Cut the thread and take the rug out of the machine.

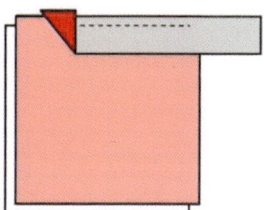

2. Now fold the binding up and away from the mug rug as shown. This will create a triangular fold in the binding at the corner.

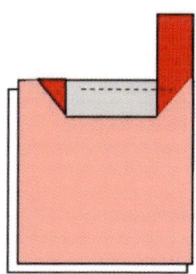

3. Hold the triangular fold (or pin it) before folding the binding down over it, aligning the edge of the binding with the side of the mug rug. Pin to secure in place. Stitch the binding along the side from top to bottom, stopping once again when you are ½" away from the next corner.

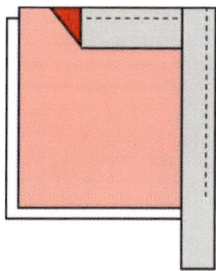

4. Repeat this process for all four corners. Continue stitching the binding until you are 1" past the beginning.

5. Fold binding to the back of the mug rug, turning under ¼" on the raw edge. Slip-stitch in place over the line of machine stitching. Make sure you do not stitch through to the front.

Hanging Corner Triangles

Some mug rugs can serve as a reminder of past happy holidays and you may wish to hang one on the wall rather than have it on your table. I am thinking of Harbourside in particular. Hanging corner triangles are a great way to hang a mug rug or small quilt using only one tack in the wall.

To create hanging corners all you need are two 3½" squares of fabric. Fold the squares in half diagonally, with WRONG sides together and press. After quilting and trimming your mug rug and before attaching the binding to your mug rug, pin the triangles to the top corners on the **back** of your mug rug so that the raw edges of the triangles match the raw edges of your mug rug.

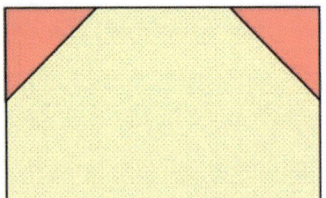 

Complete the binding using your preferred method and, as you stitch the binding in place you will also be stitching the triangles in place.

To hang your mug rug insert a batten, pencil or chopstick (trimmed if necessary) into the two corners and hang it on a small tack/nail.

Buttons, Ribbon and Trim

Mug rugs are functional mini quilts. Cups and mugs are placed on them along with cookies, cakes and biscuits. Spills and drips are unavoidable and as such, it is important that mug rugs can be laundered. Ribbons, labels and trims can add an extra dimension to little quilts but make sure they are suitable for laundering and ironing before adding them to your quilt.

It is also important that cups are steady when placed on a mug rug. Buttons seldom cause a cup to topple unless they are particularly large or have a shank. For all patterns in this book you should select only buttons that lie flat (no shank). If in doubt you should fuse and stitch a circle of felt in place of the button.

Hints and Tips for All Mug Rug Makers

You will find hints and tips throughout the patterns to help you if you are new to mug rug making or if you just wish to save some time. But here are a few of my top tips for all new, and experienced mug rug makers:

1.   If you are short of time or inexperienced at mug rug making I suggest you use a single piece of fabric for the background. Cut the background slightly bigger than needed to give you some extra room for the appliqué. You can trim it to size once you have quilted the mug rug.

2.   Measure twice and cut once. Good advice for all DIY projects – not just sewing. If you are using a directional print it will help to know that I have given all measurements in the format of "width x height".

3.   Use a neutral background for your mug rug. This will provide you with more choice when selecting the appliqué fabrics. A mug rug always looks good if the appliqué contrasts with the background. Try a soft white, cream or light grey rather than a striking white as it will be softer on the eye.

4.   Less is more. Start with three or four fabrics or colours. If you limit the fabric and colour choices your finished mug rug will appear more cohesive. As you become more familiar with the techniques and process you can play with more fabrics and patterns.

5.   Lay your fabric choices out and then leave them for a little as you make yourself a cup of tea. When you return to your fabrics, you will be able to see whether the pieces blend, contrast and work together. Another way of doing this is to squint slightly when looking at your fabric choices to see if any fabric is too bright or strong in terms of colour or design.

6.   Mug rugs only use a little fabric to make, so they provide the perfect opportunity to play with pattern and colour. Try out some unusual combinations as you never know - you might discover a colour combination or print combination that becomes a new favourite.

7.   Be careful when using stripes or checks. You will need to pay particular attention to cutting and stitching striped and/or checked fabric so that it looks good. This is particularly so with binding.

8. Let fusible webbing cool completely before cutting the shapes out – it will make it easier to peel back off the paper. I often peel back a corner of the paper after I have fused it to the fabric but **BEFORE** cutting out the shape. It helps me when peeling the paper away.

9. You may find it easier to hand appliqué your first mug rug or mini quilt unless you are confident with your sewing machine. You will find you have more control over the placement of the stitches and, if you make a mistake, it is easier to unpick.

10. Do not worry about wonky stitches or unmatched seams – only you will notice them. They also add a hand-made touch to any mug rug. Try to look past wonky stitches - look at the complete mug rug and focus on what you like most about it.

11. Mug rugs are ideal for trying out a new technique or perfecting an old one. Choose a pattern that you can remake to see how you are progressing i.e. to test your ¼" seams pick a patchwork mug rug pattern; to test your fusible appliqué technique select a pattern that uses multiple sized pieces.

12. If your batting is too thick and fluffy, place a piece of muslin over it and press it firmly with a hot iron to flatten it.

13. Use felt for very small pieces (i.e. cherries, seeds, bird beaks) – it won't fray. Felt also makes a good replacement for buttons if you are concerned the button may make a cup unsteady on the finished mug rug (see Buttons, Ribbon and Trim on page 6).

14. Have fun. Mug rugs are primarily about producing a functional little quilt whilst playing with fabric. The most you will ever lose is a few small pieces of fabric and an hour or two of your time. Smile at your mistakes – after all, they are just learning experiences. You will make fewer of them if you relax into the process.

Let us make a start on the patterns.

WATERMELON MUG RUG
(Finished size: 9" x 5½")

When the temerature rises there is nothing more cooling than a nice slice of juicy watermelon straight from the fridge. With this mug rug you can patch the watermelon flesh or use a single piece of your juiciest fabric.

Fabric Requirements:

For the Background:
One 7" x 5½" rectangle

For the Patched Sidebar
Ten 1½" squares

For the Watermelon:
Five 1½" x 4" strips of red fabric **OR** one 6" x 4" rectangle of red fabric
One 6" x 4" rectangle of green fabric
One 3" square of black fabric or felt for the seeds

You will also need:
One 11" x 7" rectangle cotton fabric for backing
One 11" x 7" rectangle of lightweight batting
8" square fusible webbing (i.e. Bondaweb/Wonderweb)
1 yard of 1¼" binding fabric (i.e. bias binding or cotton strips)

Mug Rug Construction

1. With right sides together stitch the ten 1½" squares together to create a 2½" x 5½" sidebar as shown. Press.

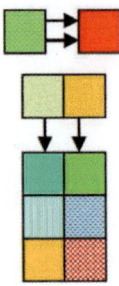

2. With right sides together stitch the patched sidebar to the side of the 7" x 5½" background rectangle to create a mug rug top measuring 9" x 5½". Press.

3. If you are patching the watermelon stitch the five red 1½" x 4" strips together along the 4" length to create a 5½" x 4" patched rectangle. You will use this patch as the fabric for the watermelon appliqué.

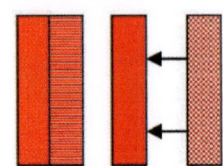

4. Trace around the watermelon flesh (red outline) and rind (green outline) from page 11, onto the paper side of the fusible webbing. Trace seven seeds. Cut out the shapes roughly - **do not** cut out accurately along the traced lines at this stage.

5. Following the manufacturer's instructions iron the fusible webbing cut-outs onto the WRONG side of your chosen fabrics. If you have patched the watermelon then you should fuse the flesh segment onto the WRONG side of your patched rectangle as shown opposite.

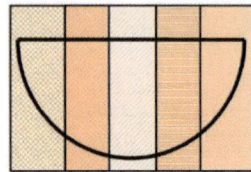

6. Allow to cool before cutting out all shapes accurately along the traced lines. Remove the paper from each shape. Using the Appliqué Sheet as a guide and ensuring the watermelon is at least ½" away from the edge of the mug rug, position the appliqué shapes onto the front of the mug rug. The 'rind' should be placed over the edge of the 'flesh'.

Tip: *You may find it easier to fuse and stitch the watermelon in place before adding the seeds. Allow for the binding when positioning the watermelon segment and place it slightly over towards the patched sidebar.*

7. When happy with the arrangement, iron to fuse in place. Hand or machine stitch the rind in place before stitching across the top of the watermelon flesh.
I used a blanket stitch but you could use any stitch you prefer.

8. Lay the 11" x 7" backing rectangle, **wrong** side facing up and place the batting on top. Position the appliquéd mug rug centrally on top with **right** side facing up. Pin the three layers together, ensuring that the backing and top remain flat and smooth. Quilt around the watermelon and along the sidebar. Add any additional quilting or stitching as desired.

9. Once all quilting has been completed, trim backing and batting to the same size as the mug rug top.

10. Bind the mug rug using the binding method of your choice. I used a 1¼" wide single-fold binding.
(See 'Binding' in General Instructions.)

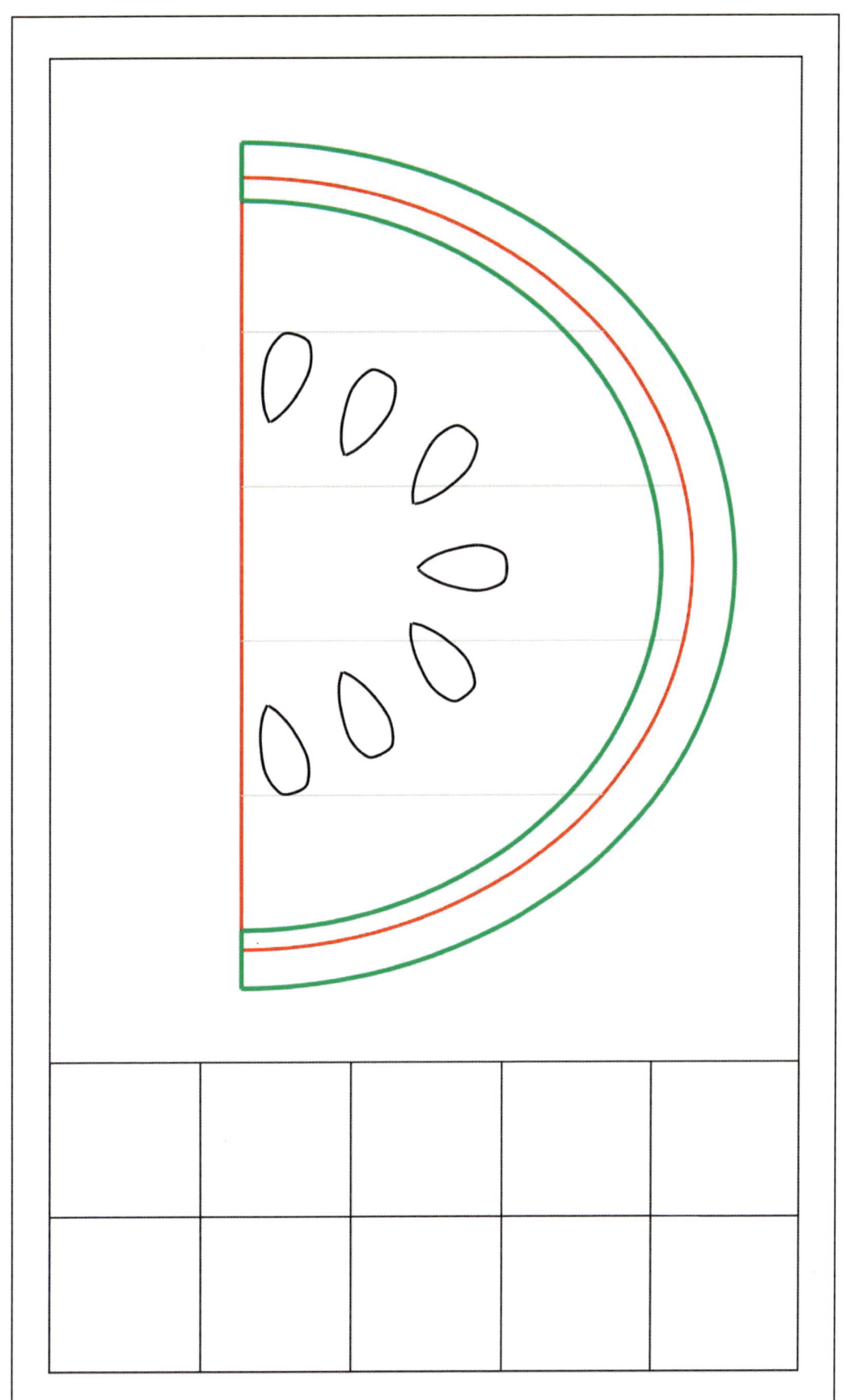

FLOWER GARDEN MUG RUG
(Finished size: 9" x 6")

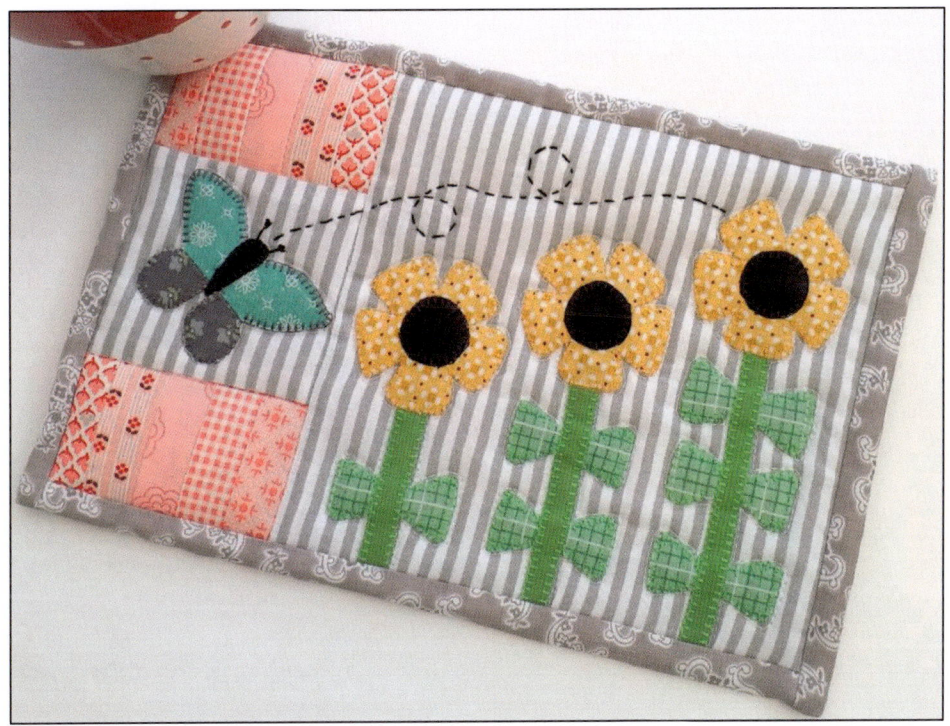

You know summer is on its way when the butterflies start visiting the flowers in your garden.
This mug rug would make a lovely gift for a gardener or nature lover.

Fabric Requirements:

For the Background:
- One 6½" x 6" rectangle
- One 3" square
- Five 5" x 1" strips from different fabrics

Flowers:
- Three 2½" squares for flowers
- Three 1½" squares for flower middles
- Six 2" x 1½" rectangles for the leaves
- One 2" x 4½" rectangle for the stems

Butterfly:
- Two 3" x 2" contrasting strips of fabric

You will also need:
- One 1½" square of fabric/felt for the butterfly body
- One 8" square of fusible webbing (i.e. Bondaweb/Wonderweb)
- One 11" x 8" rectangle cotton fabric for backing
- One 11" x 8" rectangle of lightweight batting
- 1 yard of 1¼" binding fabric (i.e. bias binding or cotton strips)
- Stranded Embroidery Cotton

Mug Rug Construction
Creating the Background

1. With right sides together stitch the five 5" x 1" strips together along the 5" length as shown below. Unit should measure 5" x 3". Press.

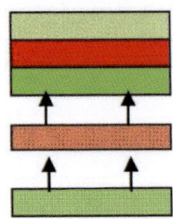

2. From this unit cut two 2" strips. Press.

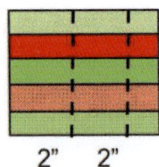

3. Stitch the two patched strips to the top and bottom of the 3" background square as shown. Press. The side unit should measure 3" x 6".

4. With right sides together, stitch the side unit to the main background rectangle along the 6" side. Press. The mug rug top should measure 9" x 6".

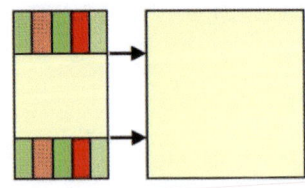

Adding the Applique

5. Create the fabric patch for the butterfly by stitching the two 3" x 2" butterfly strips together along the 3" length. Press. Use this as the fabric for the butterfly appliqué in the next step.
Tip: *Shorten your stitch length when stitching the fabric patch together to avoid the seams coming apart in the appliqué process.*

6. Trace all shapes from page 16 onto the paper side of the fusible webbing. Make sure you mark the dashed line onto the butterfly tracing as indicated on the applique page.

7. Cut out the traced shapes roughly – do not cut out accurately along the lines at this stage.

8. Following the manufacturer's instructions iron the fusible webbing cut-outs onto the WRONG side of your chosen fabrics. The butterfly tracing should be fused onto the WRONG side of the patch created at step 5, matching the dotted line on the butterfly tracing to the fabric seam of the patched unit as shown below.

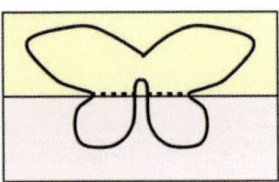

9. Allow to cool before cutting out the shapes accurately along the traced lines. Peel the paper from each shape taking care not to pull the butterfly seams apart.

10. Position the fabric shapes onto the mug rug background using page 16 as a guide. The bottom of the stems should align with the bottom edge of the mug rug and all other pieces should be **at least ½"** from the edges of the mug rug to allow for binding.

I placed the longest stem 1¼" in from the right-hand edge of the mug rug and then positioned the two shorter stems with a 1½" gap between all stems. I slipped the leaves under each stem lining them up on all three stems although you could place them on top of the stems if you prefer.

11.   When happy with the placement, iron to fuse the pieces in place.

12.   Stitch the appliqué shapes in place by hand or machine. Add any additional stitching as desired. The butterfly-line is created using two strands of embroidery cotton and a simple running stitch, as are the butterfly antennae. I added a French knot to the end of each antenna but you could use three small overstitches on top of each other.

13.   Lay the 11" x 8" backing rectangle, **wrong** side facing up and place the batting on top. Position the appliquéd mug rug centrally on top with **right** side facing up. Baste or pin all three layers together, ensuring that the backing and top remain flat and smooth.

14.   Quilt around the butterfly and the flowers. Add any additional quilting as desired.

15.   Once all quilting has been completed, trim backing and wadding to the same size as the mug rug top.

16.   Bind the mug rug using the binding method of your choice. *I used a 1¼" wide single-fold binding.*
(See 'Binding' in General Instructions.)

Butterfly
Applique Shapes

ICE CREAM SUNDAE MUG RUG
(Finished size: 9" x 5½")

When the temperature rises and you are in need of a cool spot for your afternoon treat – the Ice-cream Sundae mug rug is just the thing.

Fabric Requirements:

For the Ice Cream Sundae Background:
One 4" x 5½" rectangle

For the Patched Cherry Square:
One 3" centre square
Four 3" x 1¾" rectangles
Four 1¾" corner squares

For the Ice Cream Sundae:
Three 3" x 1¼" strips of ice-cream fabric
One 3" x ¾" strip of red (sauce) fabric
One 3" x 1" strip of red (sauce) fabric
One 2½" square of cream felt/fabric
One flat red button or a circle of felt

You will also need:
Scraps for cherries, leaf and glass base
8" square fusible webbing (i.e. Bondaweb/Wonderweb)
One rectangle 11" x 7" cotton fabric for backing
One rectangle 11" x 7" of lightweight batting
1 yard of 1¼" binding fabric (i.e. bias binding or cotton strips)

Mug Rug Construction

1. With RIGHT sides together stitch a 3" x 1¾" rectangle to the top and bottom of the 3" background square. Press. Unit should measure 3" x 5½".

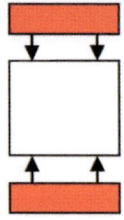

2. Stitch a 1¾" square to either end of the two remaining 3" x 1¾" rectangles to make two 5½" x 1¾" units. Press.

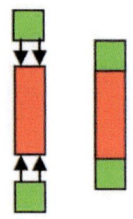

3. Stitch the patched square together as shown to create a 5½" block. Press.

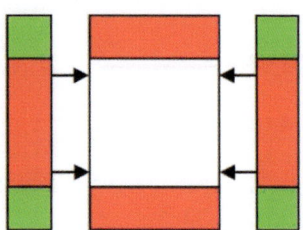

4. Finally stitch the 4" x 5½" background rectangle to the right-hand side of the patched block to create a mug rug top measuring 9" x 5½". Press.

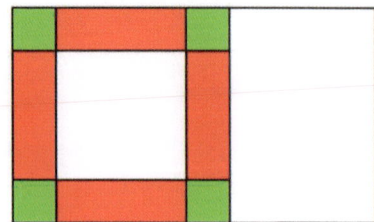

Ice-Cream Sundae

5. To make the sundae unit stitch the 3" strips together in the order as shown below. Your sundae unit should measure 3" x 3½". Press.

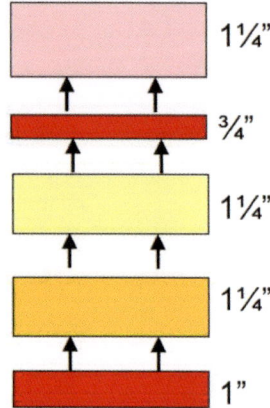

6. Trace the ice-cream sundae outline from page 20 onto the paper side of the fusible webbing making sure you mark the position of dotted 'Line A' onto the appliqué tracing. Cut out the paper shape roughly - do not cut out accurately along the traced lines at this stage.

7. Position the cut out onto the **WRONG** side of the patched unit created at step 5, lining up the traced dotted 'Line A' with the bottom seam on the unit as shown.

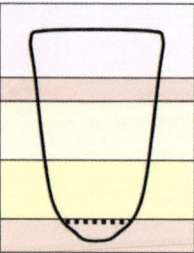

Follow the manufacturer's instructions and iron the fusible cut out onto the wrong side of the fabric. Allow to cool then cut out accurately before carefully peeling off the backing paper.

Completing the Mug Rug

8. From the appliqué sheet, trace the glass base, cherries, leaf and cream swirl onto the paper side of the fusible webbing. Cut out the shapes roughly - **do not** cut out accurately along the lines at this stage. Following the manufacturer's instructions iron the fusible webbing cut-outs onto the WRONG side of your chosen fabrics. You should fuse the cream swirl onto cream felt.
Tip: If you are using cream fabric in place of felt and you think the background may show through you can fuse two squares of cream fabric together and treat as one piece.

9. Allow to cool then cut out the shapes accurately along the traced lines. Peel the paper from each shape. Position all pieces onto the mug rug as shown on the page 20. The cream swirl should overlap the top of the ice-cream sundae very slightly. Leave **at least ¼"** between the appliqué pieces and the edge of the mug rug and remember to allow for the binding when positioning the ice-cream sundae. When happy with the placement, iron to fuse the pieces in place.

10. Stitch the shapes in place by hand or machine.

11. Create stems for the cherries using two strands of embroidery cotton and a running stitch or a chain stitch.

12. Lay the 11" x 7" backing rectangle, **wrong** side facing up and place the batting on top. Position the appliquéd panel centrally on top with **right** side facing up. Baste or pin all three layers together, ensuring that the backing and top remain flat and smooth. Quilt around the cherries and the ice-cream sundae. Add any additional quilting as desired. *I quilted in the ditch on the left-hand patched unit.*

13. Once all quilting has been completed, trim backing and wadding to the same size as the mug rug top. Bind the mug rug using the binding method of your choice. *I used a single-fold 1¼" binding.*
(See 'Binding' in General Instructions.)

14. Finally add a cherry button to the top of the ice-cream sundae or a circle of red felt.
Note: Always use a flat button unless you intend to use this mug rug for decoration only. (See 'Buttons and Trims in General Instructions.)

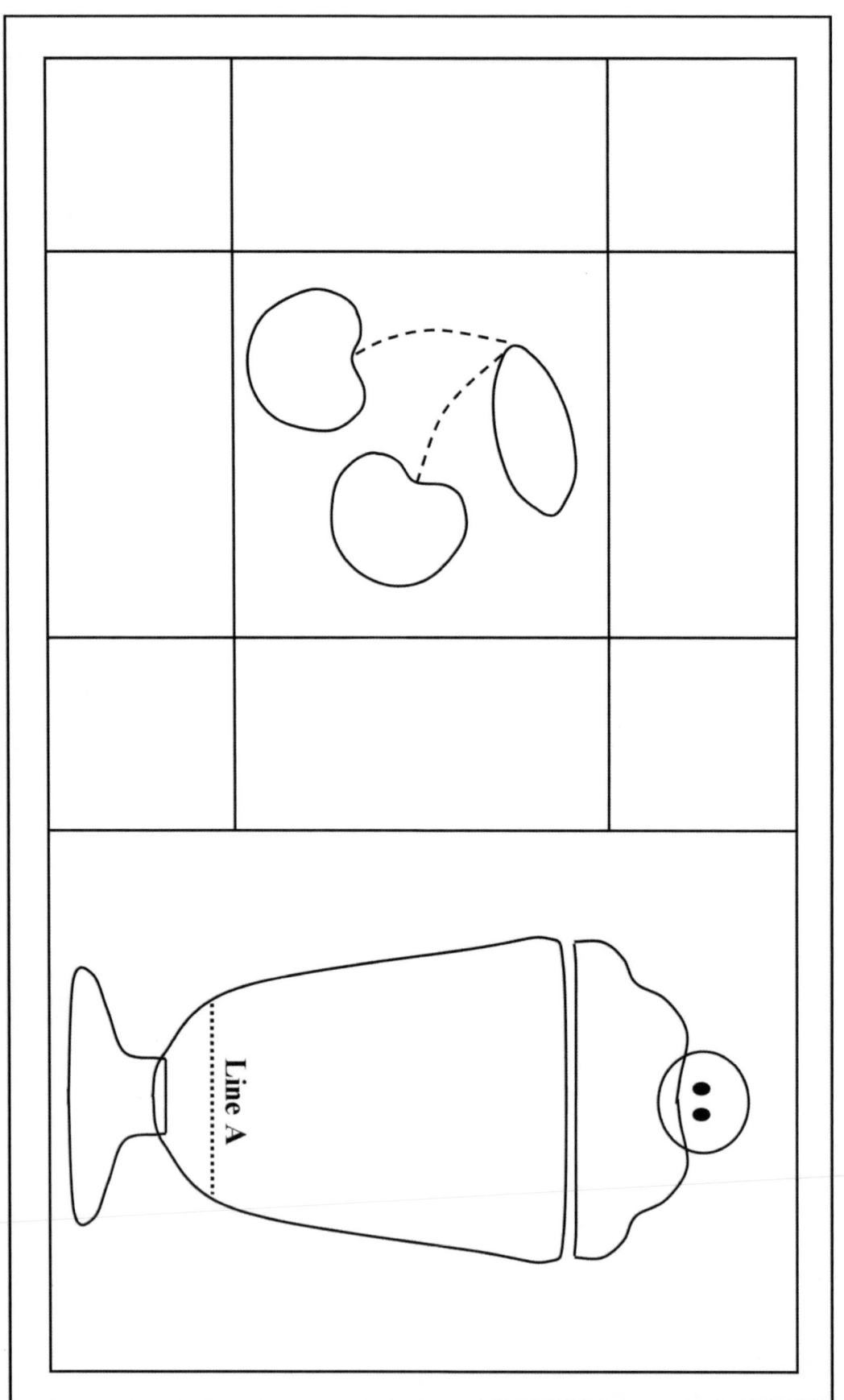

TICKER TAPE MUG RUG
(Finished size: 9" x 5½")

This 'ticker tape' mug rug is quilted as you applique the pieces into position making it a quick and easy project.
Perfect for the flag holidays and every day in between.

Fabric Requirements:

For the Background:
One 9½" x 6" rectangle
This is trimmed to size once you have stitched the pieces in place. If you are new to small quilt making cut the background rectangle to measure 10" x 7".

For the Ticker Tape pieces:
Eleven pieces from an assortment of fabric scraps.

You will also need:
One 12" x 8" rectangle of lightweight batting (see note below)
One 12" x 8" rectangle of cotton fabric for backing
One 8" square fusible webbing (i.e. Bondaweb/Wonderweb)
1 yard of 1¼" binding fabric (i.e. bias binding or cotton strips)

Note: *If you are hand stitching the applique in place you should use a natural batting that will not pull through as you stitch (flannel, cotton or bamboo).*

Mug Rug Construction

1. Trace around all appliqué shapes from page 24 onto the paper side of the fusible webbing. Cut out the shapes roughly - do not cut out accurately at this stage.

2. Following the manufacturer's instructions, iron the fusible cut-outs onto the WRONG side of your chosen fabric scraps.
Tip: Fussy cut some of the shapes for a unique and personal mug rug.

3. Allow to cool then cut out the shapes accurately along the traced lines. Peel the paper from each piece and position the fabric shapes onto the mug rug background as shown on the appliqué sheet. All pieces should be ½" away from the edge of the background rectangle to allow for the binding.
When happy with the arrangement, iron to fuse the patches in place.

4. Position the mug rug centrally on top of the 12" x 8" batting rectangle with **right** side facing up. Baste or pin the two layers together, ensuring that the batting and top remain flat and smooth.

5. Stitch around each shape by hand or machine to secure the appliqué pieces. This will also quilt the mug rug at the same time. You can use a simple running stitch, zigzag stitch or blanket stitch.
Tip: Start by stitching the largest rectangle first. Continue stitching the patches in place, working your way from the inner towards the outer patches.

6. Once all pieces have been stitched in place trim the mug rug and batting to measure 9" x 5½".

7. Place the 12" x 8" backing rectangle behind the quilted mug rug – WRONG sides together. Pin or baste the backing to the mug rug top so that both are flat and do not move.

8. With wrong sides together stitch the binding to the front of the mug rug *(See 'Binding' in General Instructions)*.
Note: *I prefer to trim the backing along each side once I have bound that side and before I bind the next side.*

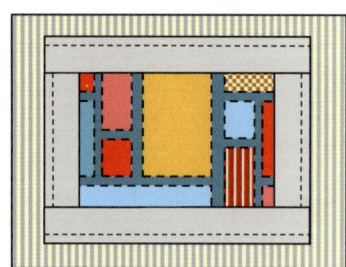

9. Trim the backing to the same size as the quilted mug rug if you have not already done so (see the note at step 8).

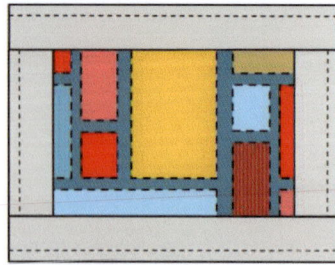

10. Complete the mug rug by folding the binding to the back of the mug rug and stitching it in place by hand or machine.

ALTERNTIVE (QAYG) METHOD

An alternative Quilt-As-You-Go (QAYG) method is to stitch through the batting **and** backing at the same time as you stitch the applique in place. However, this method will result in the stitching showing on the back of the finished mug rug. You should therefore, try to select a backing fabric that will co-ordinate with your choice of stitching thread if you do not wish it to be too prominent.

If you wish to use this method then at step 4 you should place the backing, wrong side facing up and lay the batting on top. Position the fused mug rug, right side facing up, on top of both. Pin or baste through all three layers ensuring they remain flat and smooth.

Follow step 5 to stitch all applique shapes in place, stitching through the batting and backing. Keep checking to ensure the backing is smooth and uncreased.

Once all patches have been stitched in place, trim the backing, batting and mug rug top to measure 9" x 5½".

Bind the mug rug using the binding method of your choice (see 'Binding' in General Instructions).

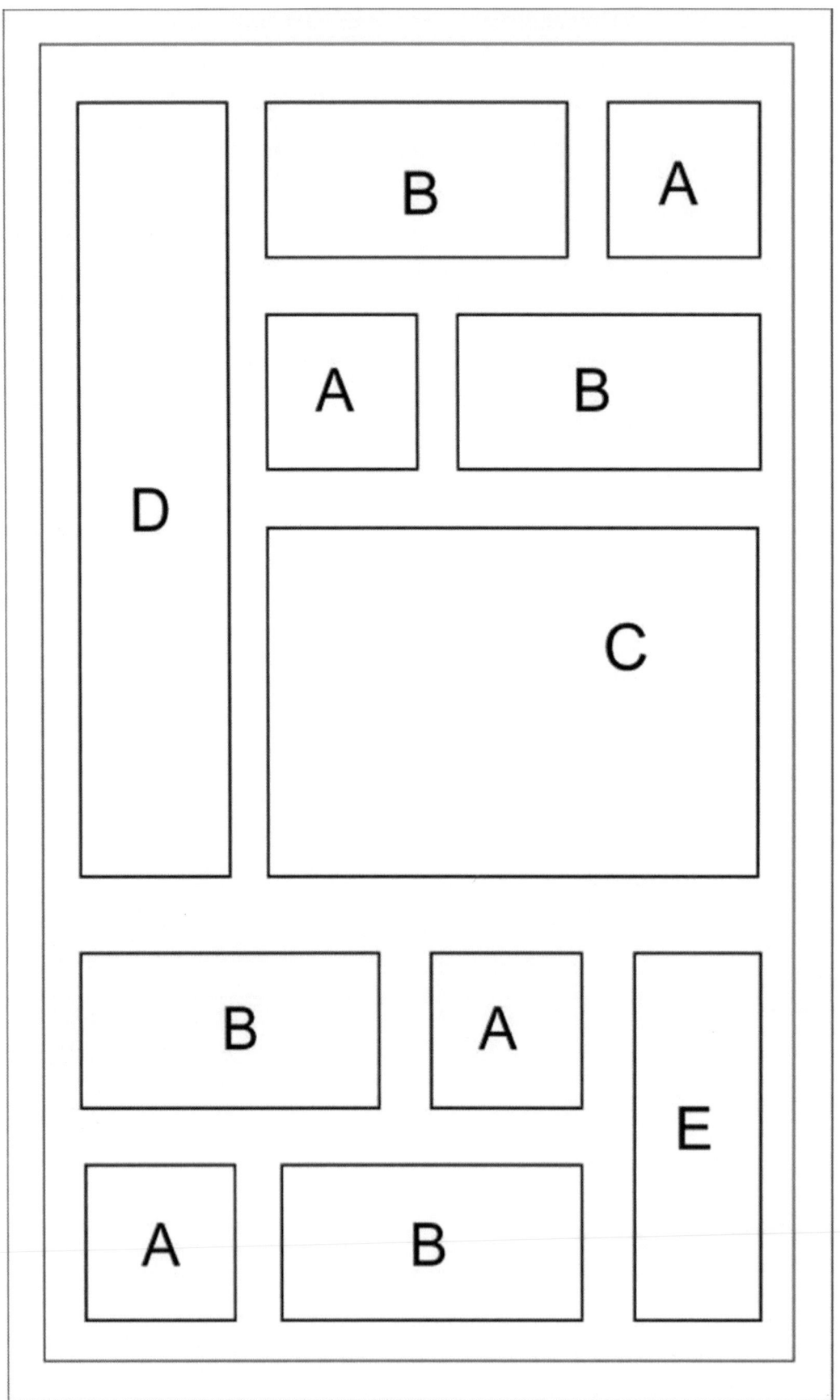

LIGHTHOUSE MUG RUG
(Finished size: 9½" x 5½")

When the summer weather is lovely a lighthouse is a great place to visit. And in stormy weather the lighthouse provides a guiding light to safer shores. Create your own safe haven for for your cup and cookie with this nautical mug rug..

Fabric Requirements:

For the Waves Section:
One 5½" square of background 'sea' fabric
A selection of 5" strips of fabric for the waves which vary in width between 1" and 1½". (*Alternatively, you can use one 6" square of contrasting fabric.*)

For the Lighthouse Section:
One 4½" x 5½" background rectangle
Three 3½" x 1" strips of blue fabric
Three 3½" x 1" strips of white fabric
Fabric scraps for door and lighthouse top.
1" square of yellow felt/cotton fabric for light.

You will also need:
One 11" x 7" rectangle of cotton fabric for backing
One 11" x 7" rectangle of lightweight batting
8" square fusible webbing (i.e. Bondaweb/Wonderweb)
1 yard of 1¼" binding fabric (i.e. bias binding or cotton strips)
Stranded Embroidery Cotton

Mug Rug Construction

1. Make the waves by stitch the selection of strips together along the 5" length to create a patched unit which is at least 6" wide. Press. (Alternatively, you can use one 6" square of fabric.)
Tip: Shorten your stitch length to patch the waves – this will stop the fabrics pulling apart through the appliqué process.

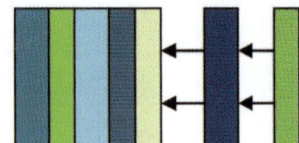

2. Trace the waves from page 28, onto the paper side of the fusible webbing. Cut out the tracings roughly, leaving approximately ¼" all the way around each wave. Follow the manufacturer's instructions to iron the wave cut-outs onto the WRONG side of the patched unit.

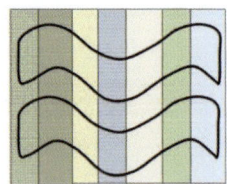

3. Allow to cool then cut out the two waves accurately along the traced lines. Peel the paper from each wave carefully, making sure not to pull the stitching apart. Position the waves onto the 5½ square of background fabric as shown. Trim the waves, if needed, to the same width as the square. Both waves should be positioned **at least** ½" from the top and bottom edges of the background square to allow for the binding.

4. When happy with the arrangement, fuse the waves into position. Stitch both waves securely in place by hand or machine.
I used a blanket stitch along the top and bottom of each wave.

5. With right sides together sew the 4½" x 5½" lighthouse background to the right-hand side of the wave block to create a mug rug top measuring 9½" x 5½". Press.

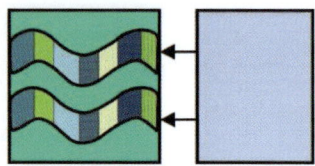

6. With right sides together stitch the 3½" x 1" strips together alternating them as shown. Press all seams towards the darker fabric. This block should measure 3½" square and will be used as your fabric for the lighthouse appliqué.

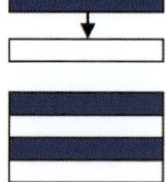

7. Trace around each lighthouse shape from page 28, onto the paper side of the fusible webbing. Cut out the shapes roughly - do not cut out accurately at this stage.

8. Following the manufacturer's instructions iron the fusible cut-outs onto the WRONG side of the relevant fabrics. The lighthouse tracing should be fused onto the WRONG side of the lighthouse block as shown.

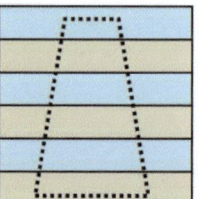

Tip: *Ensure your lighthouse tracing is straight before fusing in place. Alternatively you could position the lighthouse diagonally onto the patchwork block.*

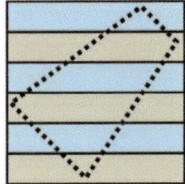

9. Allow to cool before cutting out the shapes accurately along the traced lines. Peel the paper from each shape and position the pieces onto the mug rug top as shown on page 28 and in the photo on page 25. All pieces should be at least ¼" away from the edge. Position the lighthouse slightly more towards the centre seam when placing your pieces to allow for the right-hand binding.

10. When happy with the placement, iron to fuse the pieces in place. Stitch the shapes in place by hand or machine.

11. Add detailing on the lamp using two strands of black embroidery thread and a simple running stitch.

12. Lay the backing 11" x 7" rectangle, **wrong** side facing up and place the batting on top. Position the appliquéd mug rug centrally on top with **right** side facing up. Baste or pin all three layers together, ensuring that the backing and top remain flat and smooth.

13. Quilt around the lighthouse and add any additional quilting as desired.
I quilted in the ditch between the two blocks and added shadow quilting between the waves. I also used two strands of yellow embroidery cotton and quilted light-rays extending from the lighthouse lamp.

14. Once all quilting has been completed, trim the backing and batting to the same size as the mug rug top.

15. Bind the mug rug using the binding method of your choice.
I used a 1¼" wide single-fold binding. (See 'Binding' in General Instructions.)

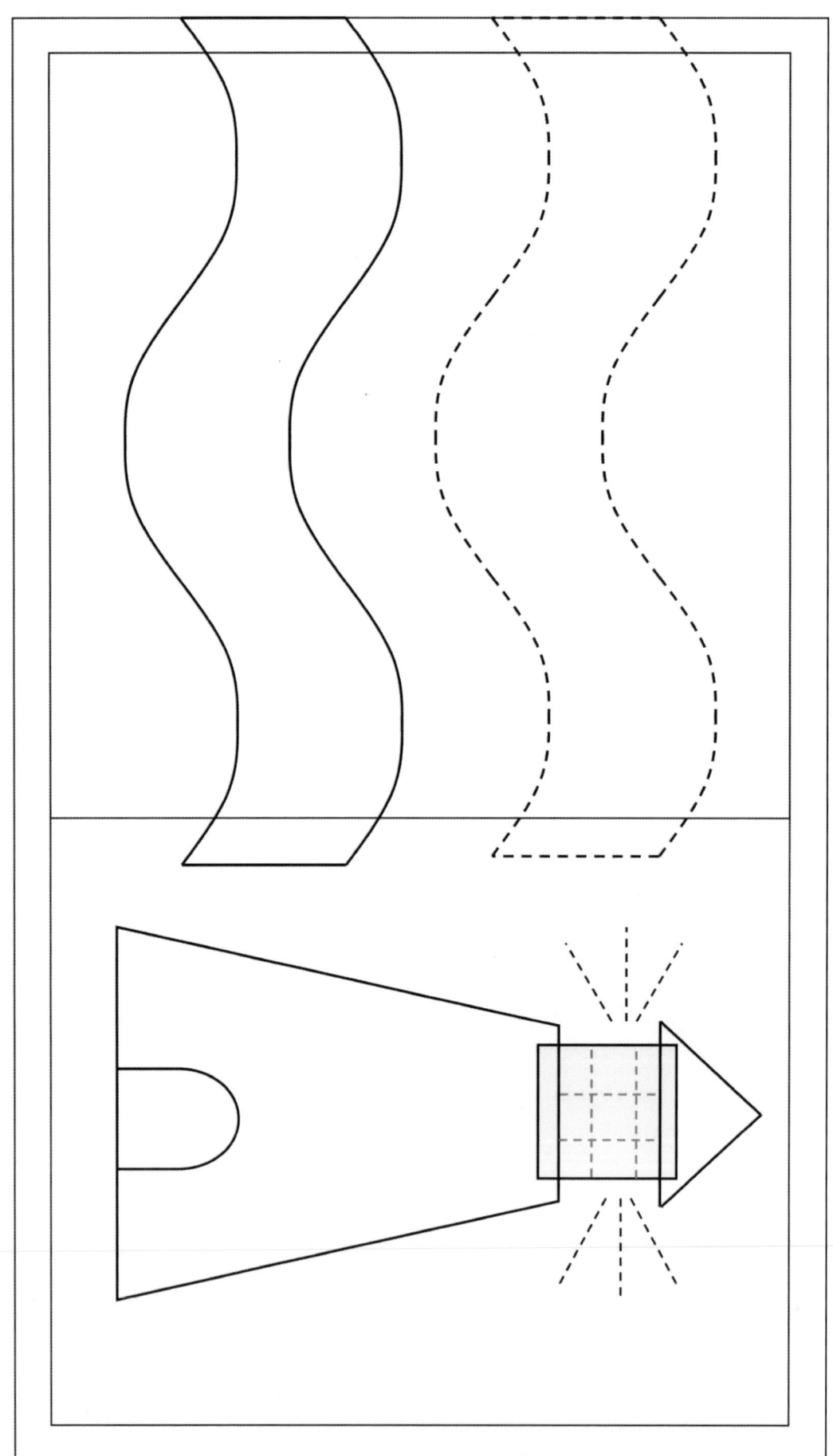

BUTTERFLY POCKET MUG RUG
(Finished size: 9" x 6")

Sometimes mug rugs are referred to as quilted cards because of their size.
Here a mug rug combines a fabric card and gift all-in-one.
And whilst it may look tricky – it really isn't.
So be at the ready with a gift that is sure to please.

Fabric Requirements:

For the Background:
One 9" x 6" rectangle

For the Corner Pocket:
One 5" fabric square

For the Butterfly:
Two 6" x 2½" fabric rectangles for the wings
One 1½" x 3" fabric/felt rectangle for the body

You will also need:
One 11" x 8" rectangle cotton fabric for backing
One 11" x 8" rectangle of lightweight batting
One 6" square fusible webbing (i.e. Bondaweb/Wonderweb)
1 yard of 1¼" binding fabric (i.e. bias binding or cotton strips)
Stranded embroidery cotton

Mug Rug Construction

1. With right sides together stitch the two 6" x 2½" rectangles together along the 6" length as shown. Press the seam open. The butterfly patch should measure 6" x 4½".

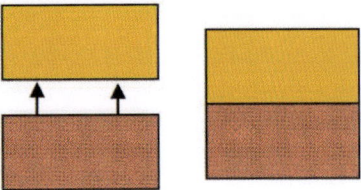

2. Trace around the butterfly and butterfly body shapes from page 31, onto the paper side of the fusible webbing (Bondaweb). Mark the position of the dashed line on the butterfly tracing. Cut out the shapes roughly - do not cut out accurately at this stage.

3. Following the manufacturer's instructions iron the fusible webbing cut-outs onto the WRONG side of your chosen fabrics. You should fuse the large butterfly tracing onto the WRONG side of the butterfly patch created at step 1, matching the line on the tracing to the seam on the patch as shown below.

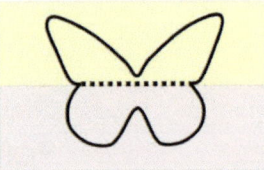

4. Allow to cool then cut out the shapes accurately along the traced lines. Remove the paper from each shape being careful not to pull the butterfly seam apart.

Creating the Pocket

5. With wrong sides together fold the 5" pocket square in half along the diagonal. Position the folded pocket onto the bottom corner of the background rectangle aligning the raw edges as shown. Pin or tack the pocket into position. You will secure the pocket in place at the same time as you bind the finished mug rug.

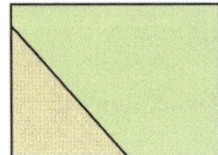 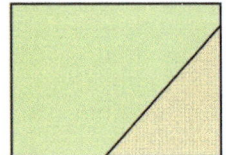

You can position the pocket on the left or right of the mug rug.

Completing the Mug Rug

6. Using the photos on pages 29 and 31 as a guide position the butterfly onto the front of the background rectangle ensuring it is at least ½" away from the edge of background rectangle and the folded pocket.
Place the butterfly body on top and add any further appliqué detail as desired.
Tip: *You can position the butterfly to sit straight as shown on page 31 or at a slight angle as shown on page 29.*

7. When happy with the arrangement, fuse the butterfly shapes in place. Hand or machine stitch around each appliqué shape to secure them.
Tip: *You may find it easier to fuse and stitch the butterfly wings in place before fusing and stitching the body.*

8. Create the butterfly antennae using two strands of black embroidery thread and a simple running stitch. Add any additional stitching as desired. *I added a French knot at the end of each antenna but you could use a simple overstitch instead.*

9. Lay the 11" x 8" backing rectangle, **wrong** side facing up and place the batting on top. Position the appliquéd mug rug centrally on top with **right** side facing up. Pin the three layers together, ensuring that the backing and top remain flat and smooth. Quilt around the butterfly. Add any decorative stitches or additional quilting as preferred.

10. Once all quilting has been completed, trim the backing and batting to the same size as the mug rug top.

11. Bind the mug rug using the binding method of your choice. This will secure the folded pocket into position. *(See 'Binding' in General Instructions.)*

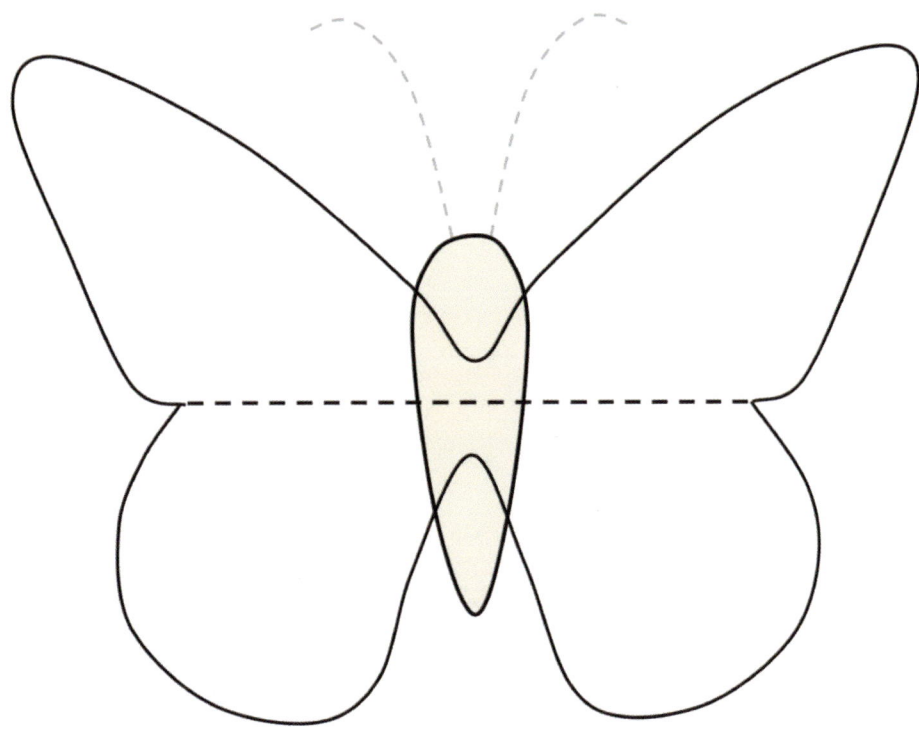

TOPIARY TREES MUG RUG
(Finished size: 9½" x 6")

In summertime in England, the big country houses open up their gardens to visitors. And it is a rare garden that doesn't include some form of topiary. Not only do visitors love to see the different shapes, the birds love to perch amongst the tightly knitted leaves.

Fabric Requirements:

For the Background:
One 9½" x 6" rectangle

For the Flower Pots:
Three 3" squares of fabric for the pots
Three 3" x 1½" of fabric for the pot rims

For the Branched Tree:
Four 3½" x 2" rectangles of various green fabrics

For the Round Tree:
One 4" square and one 3" square of cotton fabric

For the Bird's Tree:
One 3½" x 2" rectangle for the bottom branch
One 3" square for the heart
One 3" square for the bird

You will also need:
Embroidery cotton or scrap of fabric/felt for the bird's beak
One 11" x 8" rectangle of cotton fabric for backing
One 11" x 8" rectangle of lightweight batting
8" square fusible webbing   (i.e. Bondaweb/Wonderweb)
1 yard of 1¼" binding fabric (i.e. bias binding or cotton strips)

Mug Rug Construction

1. Trace around each appliqué shape from page 35, onto the paper side of the fusible webbing.
Note: You have the option of appliqueing the bird's beak (in which case trace the beak shape) or you can embroider the beak using stranded embroidery cotton – see step 7.)

2. Cut out the shapes roughly - **do not** cut out accurately along the lines at this stage.

3. Following the manufacturer's instructions iron the fusible cut-outs onto the WRONG side of your chosen fabrics.

4. Allow to cool before cutting out the shapes accurately along the traced lines. Peel the paper carefully from each shape.

5. Position the plant pots onto the RIGHT side of the background rectangle, aligning the bottom of the pots with the bottom of the mug rug. Next place the pot rims over the top edge of the pots before positioning the remaining pieces in place. Ensure that all pieces are at least ½" from the edges of the mug rug (with the exception of the bottom of the plant pots), as shown on page 35.

6. When happy with the placement, iron to fuse the pieces in place. Hand or machine stitch the shapes in place.

7. Add an eye to the bird using a simple overstitch and two strands of embroidery floss. If you are embroidering the bird's beak then create the outline using two strands of embroidery floss and three straight stitches before filling the beak with straight stitches.

8. Lay the 11" x 8" backing rectangle, **wrong** side facing up and place the batting on top. Position the topiary tree mug rug centrally on top with **right** side facing up. Baste or pin all three layers together, ensuring that the backing and top remain flat and smooth.

9. Quilt around all appliqué pieces. Create a stem for each topiary tree by machine by stitching three or four lines of stitching on top of each other. Alternatively, you could hand stitch the stems in place using 3 strands of embroidery cotton and a long stitch between each branch.
Note: *I added a stem between each branch but you could stitch just one long stem through all the branches if preferred.*

10. Add any additional quilting as desired. Once all quilting has been completed, trim backing and batting to the same size as the mug rug top.

11. Bind the mug rug using the binding method of your choice.
(See 'Binding' in General Instructions.) I used a 1¼" wide single-fold binding.

35

LADYBUGS MUG RUG
(Finished size: 9" x 5½")

Ladybugs are known as ladybirds here in England. They settle on the nettles in the hedgerow and flutter in the breeze from place to place. However, these ladybugs are homebirds and, as such, they are happy to settle on your table or workbench.

Fabric Requirements:

For the Background:
One 9" x 5½" rectangle

For the Flower:
One 5" square for the outer petal
One 4" square for the inner petal

For the Ladybugs:
One 5" square of black fabric
One 5" square of red fabric

You will also need:
Fabric scraps for ladybug dots.
One 11" x 7" rectangle cotton fabric for backing
One 11" x 7" rectangle of lightweight batting
8" square fusible webbing (i.e. Bondaweb/Wonderweb)
1 yard of 1¼" binding fabric (i.e. bias binding or cotton strips)
Stranded Black Embroidery Cotton

Mug Rug Construction

1. Trace around all shapes from the appliqué sheet on page 39 onto the paper side of the fusible webbing.

2. Cut out the shapes roughly - **do not** cut out accurately along the traced lines at this stage. Follow the manufacturer's instructions to iron the fusible webbing cut-outs onto the WRONG side of your chosen fabrics.

3. Allow to cool then cut out the shapes accurately along the traced lines. Peel the paper from each shape.

4. Position the fabric shapes onto your mug rug background using the appliqué sheet and photo as a guide. Line up the outer flower cut-out with the top left-hand corner of the mug rug as shown on the appliqué sheet. The outer petal lies slightly over the inner petal. Ensure that the ladybugs are **at least** ½" from the edge of the mug rug to allow for binding.
Tip: I found it easier to fuse and stitch the ladybug bodies and wings in place before adding their spots.

5. When happy with the arrangement, iron to fuse in place.

6. Stitch all appliqué pieces in place by hand or machine.

7. Using two strands of embroidery thread and a simple running stitch add the flower stamens and the ladybug antennae. I added a French knot to the end of each line of running stitch but you could simply overstitch for the same effect. (Optional: Add two lines of running stitch down the back of the ladybug wings).
If preferred you could machine quilt the flower stamens in place.

8. Lay the 11" x 7" backing rectangle, **wrong** side facing up and place the batting on top. Position the mug rug centrally on top with **right** side facing up. Baste or pin all three layers together, ensuring that the backing and top remain flat and smooth. Quilt around the ladybugs and around the flower. Add any further quilting as desired.

9. Once all quilting has been completed, trim backing and batting to the same size as the mug rug top.

10. Bind the mug rug using the binding method of your choice.
*(See 'Binding' in General Instructions.)
I used 1¼" single fold binding.*

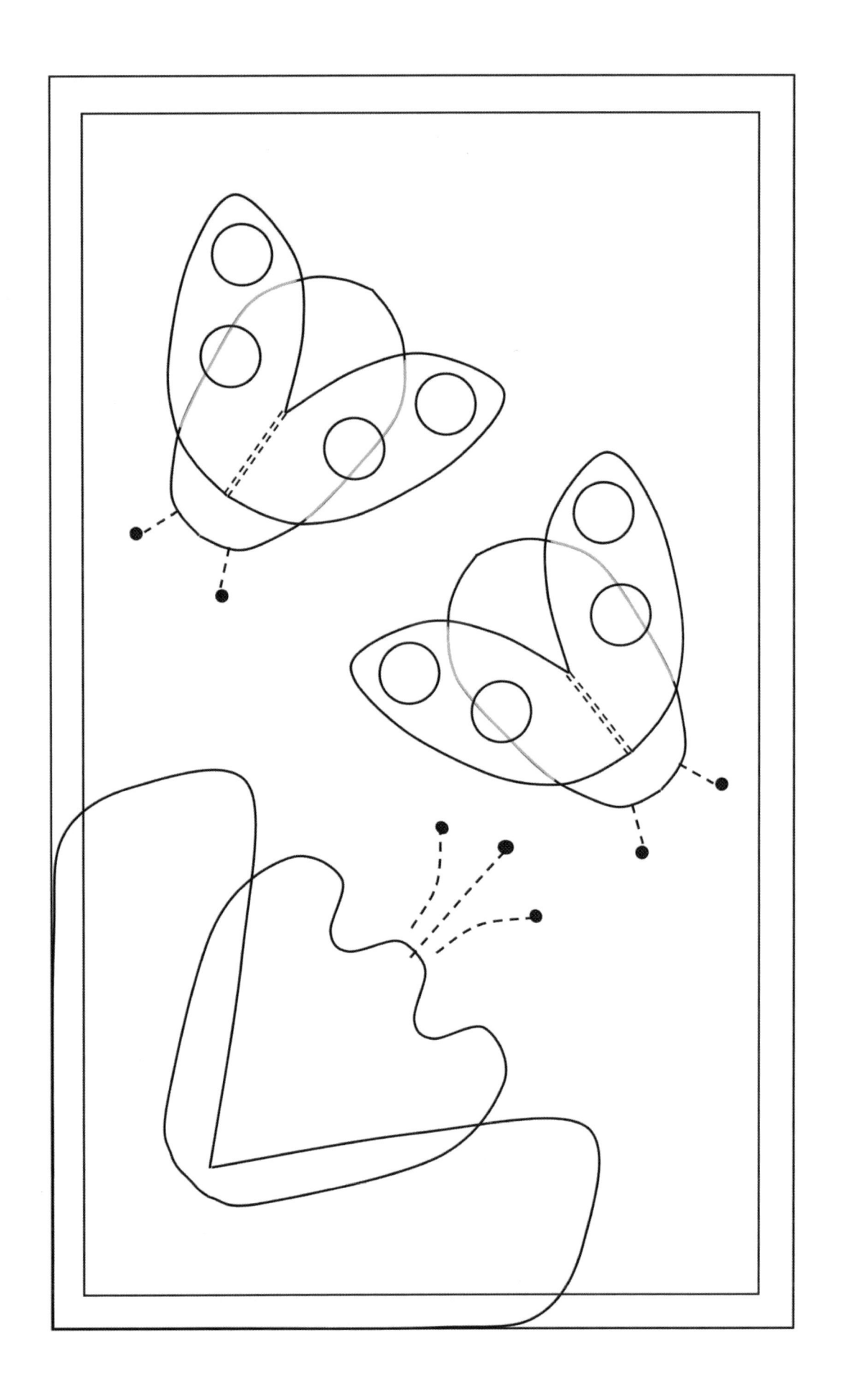

HARBOURSIDE MUG RUG
(Finished size: 9½" x 6")

Whether you spend your holidays in a little cottage by the sea or you dream of doing so, this mug rug is sure to brighten the dullest of summer days.

Fabric Requirements:

For the mug rug background:
Eighteen 1½" squares of blue/green fabric
   (OR you can use one 9½ x 2½" rectangle of sea blue fabric)
One 9½ x 4" rectangle of sky fabric

For the sea wall:
One 7" x 1½" rectangle

For each house (a total of four of each piece):
One 3½" square for each house
One 2½" square for each roof
Scraps for the doors

For the boat:
One 3" square for the hull
Two 2½" squares for the sails

You will also need:
One 11" x 8" rectangle of cotton fabric for backing
Two 4" squares of backing for hanging corners (optional)
One 11" x 8" rectangle of lightweight batting
8" square fusible webbing (i.e. Bondaweb/Wonderweb)
1 yard of 1¼" binding fabric (i.e. bias binding or cotton strips)

Mug Rug Construction

If you are using one 9½" x 2½" rectangle in place of the patched sea proceed from step 3.

1. With right sides together stitch the eighteen 1½" squares together into two rows of 9 squares each. Each row should measure 9½" x 1½". Press the seams in alternate directions for both rows (to the left on the top row and to the right on the bottom) – this will help when joining the two rows together in step 2.

2. Join the two rows together to create a sea unit measuring 9½" x 2½". Press. **Tip:** *Do not worry if your seams do not match – the finished mug rug will still look good.*

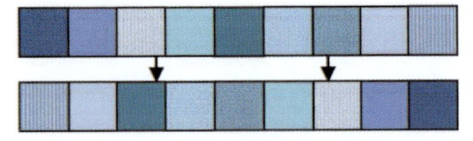

3. Trace around all the shapes on page 44 onto the paper side of the fusible webbing. Cut out the shapes roughly - **do not** cut out accurately along the lines at this stage.

3. Following the manufacturer's instructions iron the fusible cut-outs onto the WRONG side of the relevant fabrics.

4. Allow to cool before cutting out the shapes accurately along the traced lines. Peel the paper from each shape.

5. Position the hull of the boat onto the sky rectangle so that it is 1" in from the right-hand side and the bottom of the hull is aligned with the bottom of the sky rectangle as shown. When happy with the placement fuse and stitch the hull into position by hand or machine.

6. Stitch the sky rectangle to the sea rectangle, catching the bottom of the boat hull in the seam allowance. Your mug rug top should measure 9½" x 6". Press the seam towards the sea.

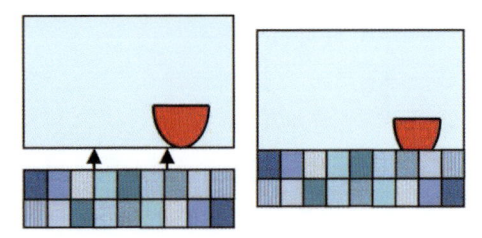

7. Now you can position the houses onto the mug rug. Use the placement diagram on page 45 as a guide. Start with the left-hand house and align the left-hand side of the house with the left-hand side of the mug rug so that the bottom of the house aligns with the sea/sky seam as shown.

8. Once the first left-hand house is in position place the remaining houses so they butt up against each other.

9. When happy with the placement of the houses, fuse and stitch them in place by hand or machine. **Tip:** *There is no need to stitch the bottom or tops of each house as these will be covered by the roof and sea wall.*

10. Once the houses are stitched, you can then position the roof atop each house and the door onto each house. Use the placement diagram on page 45 to guide you. When happy with the placement of the rooves and doors, fuse and stitch them in place by hand or machine.
Tip: T*here is no need to stitch the bottom of each door as these will be covered by the sea wall at step 11.*

11. Position the sea wall so that it overlaps the bottom of the houses and the sky/sea seam as shown on the applique placement sheet (page 45). Align the sea wall with the left-hand edge of the mug rug. Fuse and stitch in place.

12. Finally position two sails above the boat hull, leaving a small gap between the boat and the sails as shown in the placement diagram. *I positioned my sails at different heights but you may prefer to position them both at the same height.* Leave a very small gap between the sails so that you can add a mast when quilting. Make sure the sails are at least ½" from the edge of the mug rug to allow for binding. When happy with their placement, fuse and stitch them in place as before.

13. Lay the 11" x 8" backing rectangle, **wrong** side facing up and place the batting on top. Position the mug rug centrally on top with **right** side facing up. Baste or pin all three layers together, ensuring that the backing and top remain flat and smooth.

14. Quilt as preferred. I added wavy quilting to the sea before outline quilting around the top of the houses, the boat and the sea wall. I also quilted between each house.

15. Once all quilting is finished add a mast to the boat using several straight lines of stitching in brown, grey or black thread. Add a line of stitching down the middle of the wide door on the end building.
You could add seagulls to the sky if you wish using the instructions found in the Beach Huts pattern on page 48.

16. Once all quilting has been completed, trim backing and batting to the same size as the mug rug top.

17. If you want this little quilt to be hung on the wall when not in use, add Hanging Corners are detailed in the instructions on page 6. This will enable the mini quilt to be hung when not in use but will not impede with its use as a mug rug.

18. Bind the mug rug using the binding method of your choice (see 'Binding' in General Instructions.) If you are adding hanging corners as detailed in step 17, make sure to catch the raw edges of the hanging corners as you stitch the binding to the front of the mug rug.
I used a 1¼" wide single-fold binding.

HARBOURSIDE APPLIQUE SHAPES

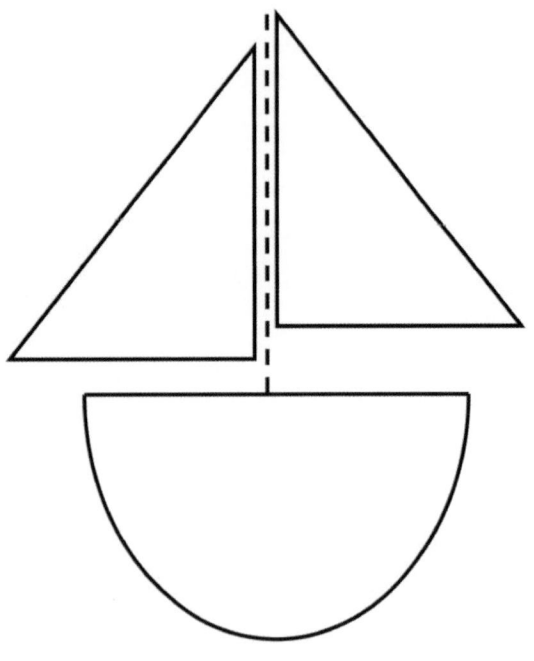

45

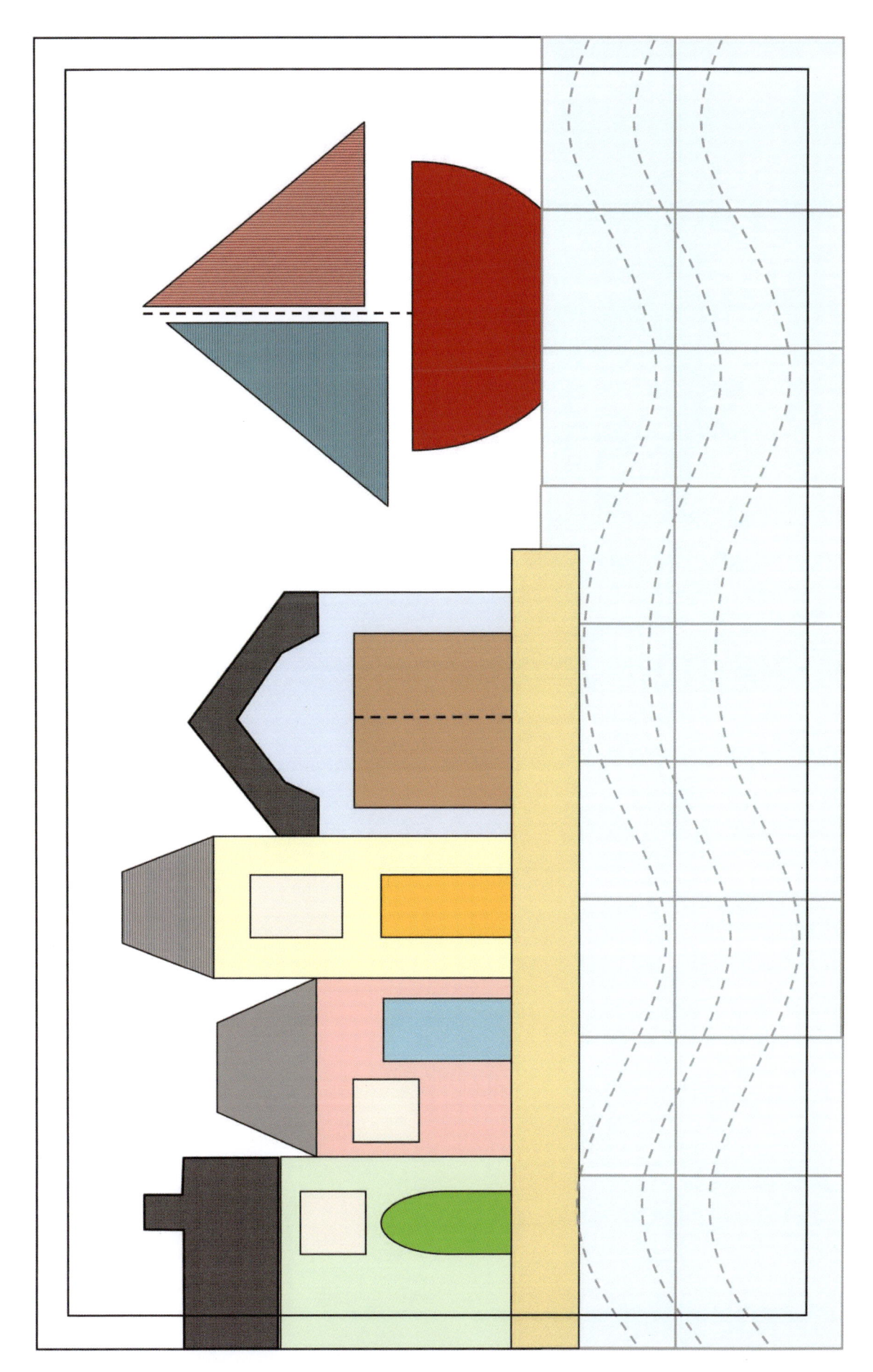

BEACH HUTS MUG RUG
(Finished size: 9" x 5½")

If the sea is a bit chilly or the wind is a bit brisk a beach hut is the perfect place to enjoy a warming cuppa and maybe a sweet treat. This colourful mug rug will provide the ideal place for your cup and cookie as you dry off and warm up.

Fabric Requirements:
For the Background:
One 9" x 4" sky blue rectangle
One 9" x 2" sand rectangle

For the Beach Huts:
Three 3½" squares

You will also need:
Fabric scraps for doors, windows, roofs and flags.
One rectangle 11" x 7" cotton fabric for backing
One rectangle 11" x 7" of lightweight batting
8" square fusible webbing   (i.e. Bondaweb/Wonderweb)
1 yard of 1¼" binding fabric (i.e. bias binding or cotton strips)
Stranded Embroidery Cotton

Mug Rug Construction

1. With right sides together, stitch the 9" x 4" blue rectangle and the 9" x 2" sand/beige rectangle together to create a mug rug top measuring 9" x 5½". Press.

2. Trace around all appliqué shapes from page 49 onto the paper side of the fusible webbing. Cut out the shapes roughly - do not cut out accurately at this stage. Iron the fusible cut-outs onto the WRONG side of the relevant fabrics.

3. Allow to cool then cut out the shapes accurately along the traced lines. Peel the paper from each shape and position the fabric shapes onto the mug rug background as shown in the photo and appliqué sheet. All pieces should be at least ¼" away from the edge to allow for the binding. When happy with the arrangement, iron to fuse all pieces in place. Stitch the shapes in place by hand or machine.
I used a blanket stitch around all shapes except for the flags and windows where I used a simple machine running stitch.

4. Using two strands of dark grey embroidery cotton and a simple overstitch or French knot create a door handle for each door. I also added two seagulls using two strands of dark grey cotton and four simple stitches for each gull as shown:

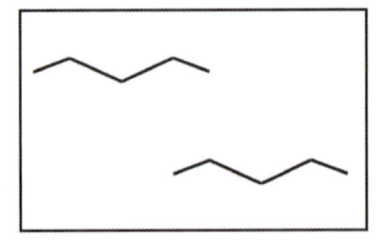

5. Lay the backing 11" x 7" rectangle, **wrong** side facing up and place the batting on top. Position the appliquéd mug rug centrally on top with **right** side facing up. Baste or pin all three layers together, ensuring that the backing and top remain flat and smooth. Quilt around each beach hut and flag. Add any additional quilting as desired.
I quilted in the ditch between the sand and the sky, under the hut roofs and I hand quilted around the bottom of the beach huts to give the sand a textured look.

6. Once all quilting has been completed, trim backing and wadding to the same size as the mug rug top.

7. Bind the mug rug using the binding method of your choice. I used 1¼" single fold binding.
(See 'Binding' in General Instructions.)

49

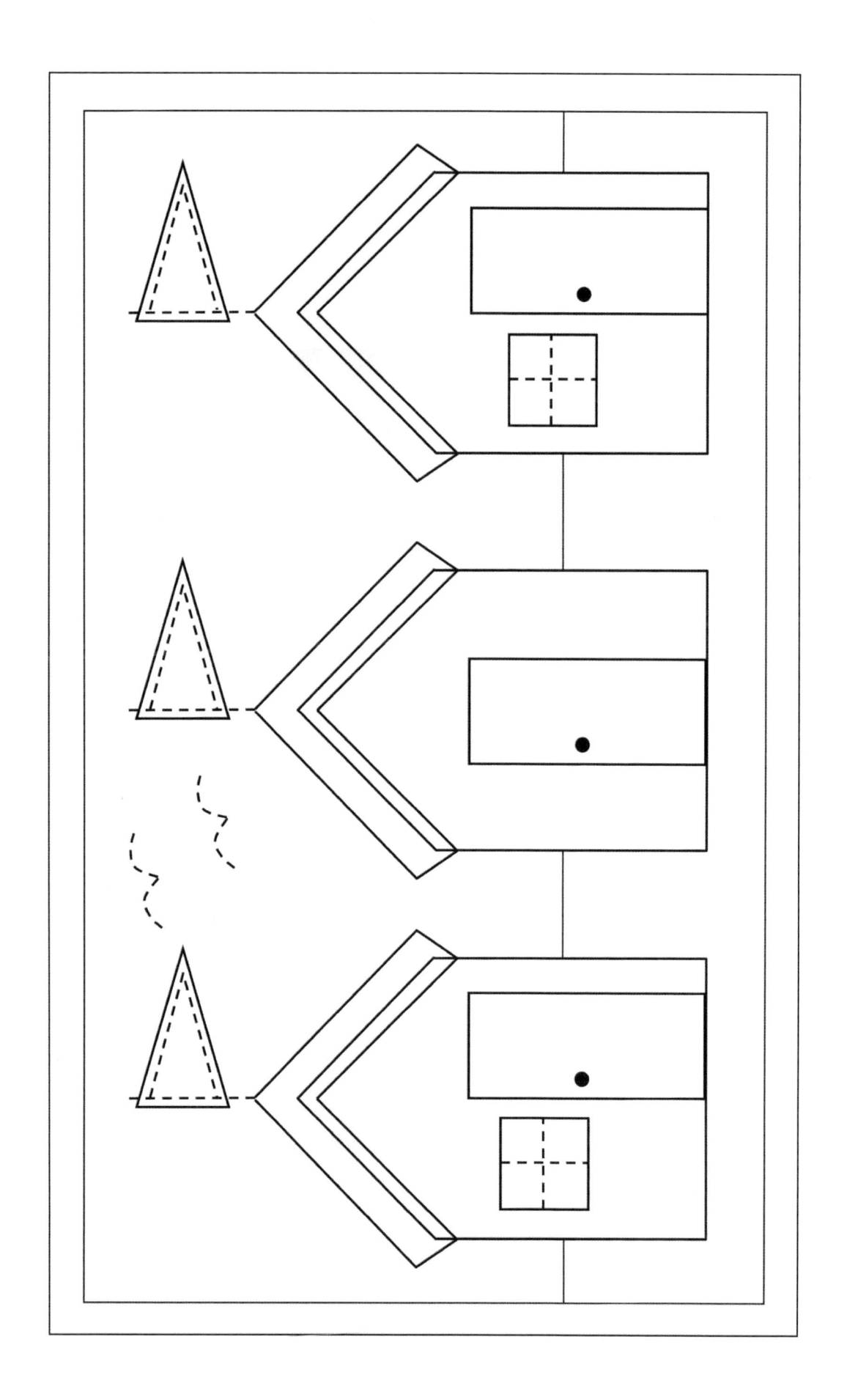

ABOUT THE AUTHOR

I am Amanda Weatherill, also known as the Patchsmith. I live in a village nestled in the Hampshire countryside where I spend my days designing and making mini quilts - they are my hobby and my passion. My philosophy is simple – share this passion so that everybody has the opportunity to create a little piece of fabric art for their home. Mug rugs are the perfect way to achieve this. Using little more than scraps of fabric you too can enjoy the hobby of mug rug making to create something unique and functional for your desk or table. In so doing you will always have a reminder close to hand of your love of fabric, fun and colour.

Join me as I share my quick and easy designs to help you create a life full of fabric, fun and friends.

You can find the Patchsmith on Etsy, Pinterest, Instagram and blogger.

To find out more about Patchsmith patterns and mug rug making visit **thepatchsmith.blogspot.co.uk**.

Printed in Great Britain
by Amazon